Dogs Do Go to Heaven!

To Karen
With Love

9/20/2010

Dogs Do Go to Heaven!

Karyn Garvin

Divine Dog Books

Also available as an eBook

www.dogsdogotoheaven.com

Divine Dog Books
5007 E. 29th Street
Tucson, AZ 85711
www.divinedogbooks.com

Names and identifying characteristics of certain individuals in the book have been changed to protect their privacy.

Publisher's Cataloging-in-Publication data

Garvin, Karyn.
  Dogs do go to heaven! / by Karyn Garvin.
    p. cm.
    ISBN 978-0-9844613-1-8
    1. Human-animal relationships–Anecdotes. 2. Dog owners–Biography.
  3. Dog owners –Anecdotes. 4. Dogs–Anecdotes. 5. Lesbians–Biography.
  I. Title.

SF426.2 .G37   2010
636.7/088/7–dc22   2010923623

Photographs on pages v, 5, 7, 21 are courtesy of the author; photographs on pages 73, 76, 81 are courtesy of Merlyn Photography.

Cover Artist: Diane Rath *www.dianerath.com*
Cover and Book Designer: Ghislain Viau *www.creativepublishingdesign.com*
Cover Art Photography: Kathleen Weinstein Photography
                    www.kathleenweinsteinphotography.com
Photo Restoration: Kevin McGuire *mcgurk1266@yahoo.com*
Book Producer: Brookes Nohlgren *www.booksbybrookes.com*

Printed in the United States of America on acid-free paper.

*This book is dedicated
to the memory of my first divine canine, Erikka.*

Mother Teresa once prayed to be a pencil in God's hands.
I offer up that same prayer.

Contents

Loving Erikka

I had always wanted a large dog, so when I graduated from junior college in 1973 and moved into an apartment with my first girlfriend, Laurie, the time seemed right. Our apartment had just been broken into, and we felt we needed to protect ourselves. We decided to each get a dog.

The next Sunday morning we looked through the newspaper classifieds. I knew I wanted a dog for my personal protection. That's when I decided I wanted a big male German Shepherd. Laurie didn't know what she wanted, but we did see an ad for Irish Setters and agreed that they were pretty. So much for our research; we set out to buy our new puppies that day.

We went to look at the Irish Setters first. Laurie took her time comparing the puppies in the litter. Finally, a male puppy seemed to win her favor. She just loved the way he looked and to her he seemed brighter than the rest. She decided then to name him Simon—the name just seemed to fit. We paid fifty dollars, which at the time was the going rate for a purebred puppy with AKC papers. Next we were off to get my German Shepherd. We ended up at a farmer's house, who kept the puppies in rabbit cages. It was nasty! The farmer told me he was all out of males but that I would be better off with a female anyway, as the female would have more of a mother's natural protective instinct. I was a little disappointed, but I decided to trust the farmer, hoping he knew what he was talking about. I pointed to one of the puppies whose coloring I liked the best. She was a sable German Shepherd. He put on his gloves and pulled her out of the cage. She was covered in dog poop! Holding her up in the air and turning her around for a quick inspection, I said, "Okay, I'll take her." That was the sum of my puppy test. I paid my fifty bucks, wrapped her in a towel so as not to get poop on me, and we headed back to the apartment to bathe them.

The days that followed were sheer bliss. When I was growing up, my family had always had dogs but I had never had my own before, and I had never really watched two puppies play. Everything they did was new to me.

Every day brought with it pure joy, making each new day feel like Christmas.

In junior college, psychology courses had been my passion. I had decided that I wanted to be a psychologist. I was fascinated with the principles of behavior modification, and now quite naturally applied them to training my new puppy. Using positive reinforcement techniques and utilizing food as a reward, I began. Wow, did it ever work! My puppy, named "Erikka" after my first childhood "best friend," was unbelievably brilliant. She loved learning as much as I loved teaching her. I know now that Erikka was heaven-sent, but then I just thought she was *brilliant*.

From the beginning, Erikka and I were one. She soon learned every command I could think of to teach her—sit, lie down, roll over, crawl, shake hands, stay, back up, and catch—mastering them all by the time she was four or five months old. She never failed to amaze me. It is believed that dogs are capable of learning at least a two-hundred word vocabulary. You could see Erikka's vocabulary expand with age. She was very special in that she listened intently to every word you said. She would cock her head and let you know, in no uncertain terms, that she understood. Even more unusual was how she would sit alongside as I talked to someone else, cocking her head and listening in on the conversation. I can still remember people noticing her as we would talk and asking, "Is that dog understanding what we are saying?"

Her fascinations in life, besides me and going places with me, were water and rocks. I could take a small rock and toss it among a million others and she would hunt and hunt until she brought that exact rock back to me. When it came to water, she was obsessed. If we were driving through the countryside and she started fussing, I could be sure there was a pond or lake just over the next hill. At a park, when I would ask her where the water was, she would find it—even a water fountain, if there was nothing else. One time we were at a laundromat when Erikka wanted a drink. She found the water fountain and looked at me. I told her, "Okay." She rose up on her back legs and reached out to rest her front paw on the fountain edge. Her paw just happened to land right on the button. The water shot out of the spigot and, naturally, she started lapping it up. She turned back to look at me, for reassurance I guess, and her paw released just enough pressure to stop the water's flow. Of course, when she turned back to drink more, her paw pressed down, and out came the water again! There were other people in the laundromat that day, observing all of this—they said nothing; I just continued doing my laundry. We all acted as if it was perfectly normal for dogs to stand up and operate water fountains just like people do.

Not long after Laurie and I got our dogs, we moved to Arizona. We had been planning the move for some time. We wanted to get away from the Iowa winters, and I was hoping for relief from my allergies. I don't think Erikka lay down once the whole trip. That was another extraordinary thing about her: she had to sit up and look out, no matter how long the trip. If I took her somewhere once, she would recognize the place immediately when we went there a second time. She loved going places. She usually sat in the front seat next to me, and I swear she knew her way around town as we drove.

Moving to Arizona was liberating for me. There was something about living in a new town that allowed me to feel free, to find myself—to be myself. Phoenix was certainly no L.A. or San Francisco, but it was definitely more accepting of alternative lifestyles than Des Moines, Iowa, was. Laurie and I searched out the gay community and I'll never forget going into my first women's bar. It had never even occurred to me that such a place even existed—a bar full of mostly young women who were gay. Now, the realization—and confirmation—that I was no longer alone, that I had a place to go and be among others like me, that I had found a new "family," made me ecstatic!

Of course, spending a lot of days in bars only added to my newly thriving drinking career. And Laurie and I were in for tough times financially, sometimes desperate times. We had arrived with little money to start with and were running out of gas money to go on job interviews. Without jobs, we couldn't get money for gas. It seemed no one wanted to hire us—they thought we were "snowbirds," a term used to describe people who visit Arizona in the winter and then leave once the rest of the country thaws out.

We ended up living out of my panel truck with the two dogs. Thank goodness for food stamps! But to qualify for them you had to prove you had cooking facilities. Well, the workers at the food stamp office were surprised to learn that they only had to step out to the parking lot to inspect our "kitchen." We qualified with our camping cooler and stove right in the truck. Finally, a convenience market chain hired us, and in no time at all, we once again had a real place to live.

Laurie and I were having relationship problems, but Erikka and I grew closer than ever. I suffered from separation anxiety whenever I left Erikka at home. It wasn't long before I started sneaking her into the convenience store with me when I worked. She would hide behind the counter and most of the customers never even knew she was there. Then again, there were those special customers for whom Erikka and I would perform. Many of my regular customers made it a habit to say "Hi" to her. My boss knew I brought her to work with me, and fortunately he let it slide. He actually liked her being behind the counter with me since working at a convenience market is a risky business.

Sure enough, it wasn't long before we were robbed. I'll never forget the day.

I bent over to do something behind the counter, and when I lifted my head, a large man was holding a gun in my face. "Give me your money!" he said. That's when I noticed his accomplice coming around the back of the counter. Erikka saw him too. She sprang up with a roar and he pointed a gun at her. "Don't shoot!" I yelled, jumping in front of Erikka and in front of the gun. He yelled back at us to "Get down on the ground," so I pounced on Erikka and told her to go down. The men warned me to stay down, which I did, and Erikka lay there frozen with me; sensing the urgency to stay put. They took the drawer from the

cash register and then they were gone. It wasn't long after that that I decided to look for work elsewhere.

I needed a place to work that would let me bring Erikka along, and then I found it—a part-time job at a guard dog service. I had the early route, which meant driving around Phoenix in the wee hours of the morning. My duties were to go from client to client—business to business—and either feed, water, and kennel the dogs that had been out all night or pick up our dogs and return them to our kennel so that the businesses could open. Erikka made it her job to sit next to me in the front seat and learn the route as well.

My first night on the job I was in training, so I got into the truck to ride with the driver whose shift I would be taking. Around the kennel, it was the topic of conversation that I would be taking over the "Doberman" route.

"What's the big deal?" I asked.

"You'll see," warned the driver.

Sure enough, we pulled up to the business where the Dobermans lived and worked. It was a male and female dog team, which was typical at our locations. Male and female teams usually worked better together. As a rule, the female is the more vocal of the two, sounding off if there's anything to be concerned about. The male determines if he should get involved, and if he chooses to do so, he'll move in, push the female out of the way, and take over. As soon as our truck pulled up, the pair came running up to the fence. Once they were certain it was us—the guard dog service coming to take care of them—the fight broke out ... before the driver even had time to get out of the truck.

I watched as the guy grabbed a snare off the truck and rushed towards the gate. He was a nervous wreck, trying to unlock the gate and get in there before the dogs did serious harm to each other. Once inside, he started hitting them and then pried them apart with the stick. When the fighting stopped, he went about his business— cleaning up after them, changing their water, and putting out new food. They were plenty happy to have him there and followed him around. Sure enough though, just as he was getting ready to leave, the fight broke out again. The driver started all over again, hitting and prying, and didn't leave until he succeeded in separating them again. All the while, I had waited in the truck, just as he'd instructed. But watching this scene, I knew intuitively that the dogs were seeking his negative attention. I decided then and there that I would certainly handle it differently.

Within a few nights, I had the shift to myself. The Dobermans acted out the same scenario, as if they had been primed for my arrival. I ignored them, took my time and just went about my duties. As soon as they realized I didn't care to get involved, the fighting stopped. Plus, they wanted to come and see who this new person was.

Of course, when I started to leave the fight broke out again. I simply left. By the third or fourth night, when the dogs had not been given any attention for fighting, they stopped, and we were able to spend more time just enjoying each other. It really is true that 95 percent of all dog fights only occur when people are present. It's the people's reactions that make fighting so rewarding for the dogs.

Erikka loved our job. She sat next to me in the front seat and learned the route as I did. Often, when I'd show up to kennel the dogs, they didn't want to go back in, even though their reward for kenneling up was getting fed. I would drive up to the exterior fence. Most locations had a gate where I could enter the kennel, clean up the area, and leave food and water. Then I could step back outside and unlock a lever that opened a dog door which allowed them back into the kennel so that the business could open. Many of these dogs were too dangerous to touch, but they had a good life overall. For the ones that repeatedly gave me a hard time kenneling, I would call on Erikka. She knew the routine. As soon as we pulled up she knew if this was one of the stops where her help would be required. She would bound out of the truck and run to the fence, barking furiously at just the right time and place. The dogs would come running into the cage to bark back at her. As soon as she heard the lever latch, we were both back in the truck and off to the next stop. She was a huge help.

It wasn't long before Laurie and I decided to go our separate ways. We had been together as partners for approximately four years. There were, however, some irreconcilable differences and it became clear that it was time to move on in different directions. She kept Simon, and Erikka and I started rooming here and there. Eventually, we rented an apartment that was conveniently located right across the street from my favorite women's bar.

The bar's owner had picked up on how extraordinary Erikka was and let me "sneak" her in. Inside the bar, next to the front door, was a pinball machine. I would have Erikka go and lie down under it. She was content to just stay there for hours. She never broke her stay nor did she ever try to wander through the bar looking for me. The bar could be packed with hordes of people going in and out at the same time. The only time she would get up automatically was if I was among the crowd that was leaving. It never failed to amaze me how I *could not* sneak out without her knowing. There was no tricking her. I still wish I knew how she knew.

One day I came home to my apartment, and she wasn't there. My next-door neighbor had accidentally let her out, and she was gone. I was frantic looking for her, and then it occurred to me to try the bar across the street. Sure enough, I found her under the pinball machine, waiting for me. Pathetic, but true!

Erikka and I were connected on the soul level. She was my soul mate. I could look at her and just know what she wanted and she could look at me and know the same. There was nothing on earth more important to me than her, and the same went for her, I'm sure. We would just sit together and she always wanted me to hold her paw; it was her way of holding hands. I can still remember the look and feel of her foot, her leg, her ears, her eyes. Most of all, I remember how it felt just to be together. She was a daughter to me. She was also my guardian. With age, she appointed herself a new responsibility, that of keeping people away when I was asleep. I certainly never taught her that; it was something that just came naturally to her and I loved it. Those who needed to wake me didn't appreciate it very much, but Erikka was the only one allowed to do the waking.

Erikka was there for me. Drinking and smoking pot the way I did back then was a way for me to try to feel better. The initial fun feeling I got when I only drank or smoked once in a while disappeared rapidly when it became a part of daily life. I was a pothead. When drugs dull the pain, they also dull the joy. Soon I started to feel dead inside. Back then, it wasn't hard for me to slip back into suicidal thoughts, especially since I had had so much practice thinking that way as a kid.

In 1963, when I was in the third grade, my father applied for an overseas transfer with Firestone Tire and Rubber Company. He was assigned to Bombay, India. Little did I understand the life-altering adventure I was about to begin. My father's position there lasted for approximately three years. Families from all over the world were temporarily stationed in Bombay, many from the United States, and it was among these families that we made our closest circle of friends. It was also understood that we would have to say goodbye to everyone when it came time to leave. Only our Indian friends were there permanently. As we were getting near the end of our stay, I began dreading the day I would have to say goodbye. Those were the closest friends I'd ever had. Having to say goodbye to my best friend Erica was almost unbearable.

I'd made friends with plenty of other girls, with whom I had great times, and nothing even resembling a crush ensued. But with Erica everything was different. Erica and I had tons in common—and we were inseparable. There was no confusion or awkwardness between us. We were absolutely, unconditionally, sincerely "best" friends. Yet I knew in my heart that she meant more to me than that.

I was twelve years old when we moved back to Des Moines. I missed Erica so much; I wrote to her nearly every day. I needed to see her again. I obsessed on how and when it would happen ... trying to calculate how many lawns I would need to mow to save up enough money to visit her now that her family had returned to California. When I began to see how much she meant to me—and heard myself in those letters—I realized that I was in love ... in love with my best friend. What a shock! What did it mean? Only that I was unfortunately, helplessly, unthinkably homosexual. It wasn't long before she stopped answering my letters. She had moved on like any normal kid would. And eventually I moved on too. But not without considerable pain.

In junior high, I met Diane, who became my new best friend—and the same thing happened. This should have been one of the best times of my life. When you're in love at that young age, it's everything. There's nothing more important in the whole world. But, instead, here I was in a horrible trap. I had all these incredible feelings like I had had for Erica, and once again, I couldn't tell anybody. I certainly couldn't tell Diane! In the late sixties, everything you could find to read about homosexuality described it as deviant behavior and a mental illness. I didn't really believe I was mentally ill, but I realized the rest of the world would say I was ... if they knew. And I believed that I was the only one who felt the way I did. My life grew hellish from that point on. Every night became a time of misery in which I cried for hours, muffled by my pillow, in my lonely room. In fitful sleep I had nightmares of being taken away and locked up. I knew I would never marry a man, and I believed that no female would ever truly love me.

I became a wild child. I stopped caring about grades or making my parents proud. I took up smoking, drinking, and using other drugs. Things would never change, so what did it matter? If I was lucky, an overdose, a car accident, or something else would end my torture.

Finally, after graduating from high school and enrolling in junior college, I met Laurie, who lived across the hall in my dorm. Soon Laurie and I became best friends and, yes, I fell in love with her. The big difference this time was that Laurie loved me back, and in my second year of junior college I entered into my first loving relationship.

What a difference that made! Finally, I knew that love could be wonderful. I could love and be loved. I felt alive, and life was suddenly worth living. I felt God's love too. For a time, the countless hours of pain and suicidal thoughts were in the past, though using recreational drugs would stay with me for years to come.

Through the difficult times after Laurie and I split up, it was Erikka who kept me alive. At times I wanted to leave this planet, but there were a few things that kept me from taking that final step, like not wanting to hurt anyone I knew. Most of all, I knew I couldn't leave Erikka behind, which meant I would have to take her with me. But there was no way I could take her life. Because of my love for her, it was easier to just stay alive.

Little by little, sometimes almost imperceptibly, my life began to get better. Fortunately, the hours I worked at the guard dog service allowed me to go back to school during the day. And at that time, lucky for me, my parents were happy to help with my tuition. So I started classes at Arizona State University, and of course Erikka did too. Some instructors let me bring her into class. Otherwise, I left her playing outside at a big brick fountain in the center of campus. There were always students sitting around its wide edge. All it took was the fountain and a stick to entertain Erikka. She was good at making friends and had a way of getting someone to throw the stick for her. Even if they weren't interested initially, she was persistent. It was good enough entertainment for an hour. Erikka was well-known and liked on campus. I was not the only kid who brought a dog to school, but it was a different world then.

One day, at the start of a new class, I had to go to a particular science building where they didn't allow dogs. I told Erikka to wait outside. I went in, and after some searching found the correct classroom on the third floor and took my seat. It wasn't long before I heard toenails tapping down the aisle. How had Erikka found me? It was like she had psychic radar. Could it have been her keen sense of smell? Clearly, she hadn't been running through the building from room to room or floor to floor looking for me. If she had, she would have been escorted out. No, she came straight up the stairs, right to the correct room, and down the very aisle where I was sitting. I was thrilled and annoyed with her at the same time. I quickly had her lie down beside me, and she knew I was irritated. She moved in as close to me as she could. How wonderful—and embarrassing. I used my foot to gently push her away a little, and she let out a big loud moan as if to tell the whole room I had pushed her. She was very good at communicating whatever it was she wanted people to know.

The job with the guard dog service grew tiresome after a few years. I had learned many valuable lessons about kennels, dog behavior, and protection training that I would take with me, but I was ready for something more challenging and certainly more prestigious. I saw an ad in the paper and applied for a job with a dog training company in Phoenix. The man who owned the business was so impressed with Erikka that he hired me strictly on her performance. She gave a great obedience and protection demonstration for him. Back then, most people wanted their dogs trained for both.

My new boss, Mike, offered me no formal training. He just started giving me customers. I was to go to their homes and teach them how to train their dogs. He did recommend a few books, though, which I read before I went to my appointments. At that time, in the mid-1970s, the most popular book on the subject was *The Koehler Method of Guard Dog Training.* It had been on the bestseller list and was also awarded Best Dog Book of the Year. The way I had trained Erikka—using food as a reward—was not a popular method then. In fact, I often heard things like: "Don't use food as a reward—that's bribery," or "The dog needs to perform just because you say so," and "You need to establish dominance over that dog."

Bill Koehler was a military man and he made a huge contribution to the dog training world. His attitude about obedience being a dog's job and verbal praise being reward enough was influenced by the requirements for military working dogs. Though it went against the methods of the time, I went ahead and slipped in food rewards anyway. I still thank God for Bill Campbell's book *Behavior Problems in Dogs.* This book set a new precedence in the approach to behavior problems and was my bible for a very long time. Yet most of what I learned about training dogs, and teaching people to train their dogs, came from actually doing it in the real world. As Mike assigned me clients whose dogs had behavior problems, I also had the opportunity to apply everything I knew about psychology and behavior to come up with my own training style. I had both the need and the freedom to be creative.

Erikka went with me on training appointments, and I used her in every way I could. As time went on, I went from being a trainer to being a training consultant. I would go to the owners' homes on the initial appointments, find out what their needs were, and sign them up for training. At some point during every free consultation, I would bring Erikka in, or take the owners outside to her, and we would demonstrate what their dog would be learning. She loved her job! She was perfect almost 100 percent of the time. The only problem was that she knew the routine too well. On one occasion, I noticed—as did the customer—that as soon as he tore the check from his checkbook, Erikka jumped up and ran to the door, as if to say: "You got the check. Let's go!" The customer gave me a piercing look and said, "Boy, you've got that dog well trained!"

In Erikka's sixth year, I started thinking about the fact that she was getting older. Attached to her as I was, I dreaded the thought that one day I'd be without her. So, I got another German Shepherd puppy and named her Ingrid. Ingrid was a very different dog. From the start, she was totally fixated on Erikka: she was as bonded to

Erikka as Erikka was to me. Poor Ingrid was less than a year old when she came down with Valley Fever, and it hit her hard. Valley Fever—coccidiomycosis— is endemic to California's Central Valley, Southern Arizona, and parts of New Mexico, and is caused by fungal spores found in the soil and in blowing dust.

Certain people and animals are more susceptible to it than others. When Ingrid contracted the disease, the treatment in use today was only in the experimental stages and not available to help her. I realized Ingrid was dying, slowly and painfully. When she became paralyzed in her hind quarters, and in such pain that she would snap at me if I went to move her, I knew the kindest thing I could do was to take her in to the vet and have her put to sleep. Even though I knew this was the right thing to do, it was one of the hardest decisions and most difficult actions I had ever had to take. Usually when you do the right thing it automatically feels good. But not this! It takes a lot of justification to be able to come to peace with euthanasia, particularly when you really don't know what happens to your pet after they die.

To make matters worse, just before Ingrid got so very sick, my Erikka was diagnosed with the same disease, Valley Fever. I was devastated. Fortunately, Erikka remained quite healthy until her last day. There were mornings when I knew she wasn't feeling well, but she still wanted to go to work with me anyway. Maybe it was one of the things we had in common: our work was a big part of our self-worth. She loved her job. But then it came, that morning when I woke up, looked at Erikka, and could tell right away that she had taken a turn for the worse. I remember my panic. I called the veterinarian and made an appointment to take her in at once. But, before bundling her into the truck, I called a well-known animal communicator I had worked with in the past. I had spoken with her about Erikka once before, and somehow I knew she would help me.

When I first heard about people who had an uncanny ability to communicate with animals, I had been skeptical, but having used their services, I had become a believer. Many of them work closely with veterinarians as they can "sense" how the animal is feeling, where it is hurting, and help the veterinarian to locate the problem. This particular

woman could also communicate with pets and help their owners over the phone. Distance made no difference. When I called her and told her what was going on, she agreed that I should cancel all of my appointments for the day and stay with Erikka.

Off to the vet we went. The doctor was clearly concerned when she saw Erikka, but could not tell exactly what was going on. She drew a blood sample and gave her a huge injection of vitamins as an interim measure. I could tell that Erikka felt better almost immediately.

As we drove back home to wait for the results, Erikka was obviously happier, sitting up and looking out the truck window. At the house, I tried to make her comfortable. She had always had a thing about keeping her eye on me every second, so I made a bed for her on the couch and positioned it in the middle of the living room so she could see me wherever I went. I made sure to not be out of her sight for long, as I didn't want her to have to come looking for me.

Sadly, the improvement from the vitamin shot was short-lived. As the day wore on I kept checking on her; I could see she was feeling worse by the hour. She was gradually losing her ability to move. And she was going blind. As time passed she could barely lift her head, and I too was almost blind with tears. I was humbled, powerless, and we were both completely in God's hands.

Down on my knees, kneeling in the center of the living room, I cried and prayed. My precious Erikka was dying and I prayed for God's help. "Please God, I know that You are the only one who can save her." It was in that moment, for the first time in my life, that I actually heard a voice. I heard these words: "SHE WILL BE REPLACED WITH SOMETHING MUCH GREATER." Where did those words come from? The voice was loud and clear. I looked around the room in wonder, trying to see who had spoken those words. They weren't my words. Replacing Erikka was certainly the last thing I had on my mind at that moment. But this experience temporarily shocked me out of my panic and grief.

Around nine o'clock that evening my girlfriend, Cindy, who was also my partner at that time, came home from work. She took one look at Erikka and knew that this was it. By this time, the poor dog was almost totally blind and unable to even lift her head. Once again, my panic set in. I had to do something!!! Grasping at straws, I called the animal communicator again, not really thinking she would answer the phone at that time of night since she had strict office hours. To my amazement, she did pick up.

"Yes, Karyn."

I hadn't said a word, but she knew it was me. I told her Erikka was dying and I really didn't know what to do.

"You know, when you called this morning, I felt she was, but I didn't want to say that over the phone until I was sure."

"Karyn," she continued, "do you believe in heaven?"

"Yes. Why?"

"Well, it might help you to know that dogs do go to heaven, too!"

"What?"

What kind of story was she about to tell me? I certainly didn't feel like listening, but she persisted. She told me that when dogs are very near death, they see this big green grassy hill with a bright white light behind it. When they go over the hill, they enter into heaven. And I'm thinking, "Yeah, what is she talking about? How does she know?"

She continued: "Karyn, whenever a dog dies, a dog it has known in its lifetime comes down to lead it up over the hill. Right now, you have a little, mostly black, female German Shepherd there with you to lead the way for Erikka."

"You mean Ingrid?" I asked.

Immediately, upon hearing that name, Erikka started screaming and throwing her body forward, struggling to sit up. She did this over and over.

"Erikka, is Ingrid here?"

And she screamed again, still trying desperately to sit up, saying to me as clearly as if she spoke English, "YES, YES! INGRID IS HERE!"

I got it! I was astounded! I had never mentioned anything to the animal communicator about Ingrid, and Ingrid, who had died approximately a month and a half before, was indeed a mostly black, little female German Shepherd. I got off the phone in total amazement. Of course, to test what I had just heard, I asked Erikka one more time, and again she told me, in no uncertain terms, that yes, Ingrid was there.

Still not satisfied, still desperate to save her, I called the veterinarian at home. She answered the phone and I told her, "This is it. She's dying. What are we going to do?" We talked for a moment and then I said, "Shall I bring her in and maybe you can give her another shot?" Suddenly Erikka started screaming at me again. This time she was saying, "NO! NO! NO!" and it was only when I told her, "It's okay, you can stay," that she relaxed.

The veterinarian heard her screaming over the phone and cried, "My God, Karyn, is that her?" I said yes, and she intuitively knew what Erikka was telling me. She said, "Karyn, you've got to let her go!" That was it. I got off the phone. I knew the time had come. There was nothing more I could do. I lay down beside Erikka. She really did not want to go. But I told her, "It's okay, you can go now." She was terribly tense, so I started calming her with my voice, telling her to relax. Speaking quietly to her, I soothed her into a relaxed state and she slipped away. Sure that she was gone, I sat up, but suddenly she came back. So once more, I went through the whole process of relaxing her, and the next time I felt her slip away, I just lay there and stayed still until she was gone.

Finally I sat up. This time it was different. God was everywhere in that room at that moment. And as sad as I was, I had a strange sense of joy. Erikka had made the transition into the Light, and God was there, everywhere. I didn't go to bed sad that night; on the contrary, I was full of peace. I was overwhelmed, astounded by the miracle of God's presence, and by all that had been communicated to me. Of course, when I woke up the next morning, I held Erikka close to me, and sobbed for hours. I cried like I have never cried in my lifetime.

Years later I was involved in a seminar put on by the Shanti Foundation, an organization that operated as a support system for people who were terminally ill. Completing the seminar qualified you to be a volunteer for the organization. In it, they taught you about the concerns and feelings of someone near death, so that you, in turn, could be a good support system. You can well imagine the gravity and sadness that training of this sort would bring up for those attending. I thought I was faring quite well through the program until they showed a video of people, who were very near death, being interviewed. Over and over again, the dying reported experiences such as seeing a deceased relative standing at the foot of the bed, knowing the relative had come to show them the way. It was during this video that I burst into tears as I heard from the lips of humans what Erikka had told me so many years before.

I know for certain that dogs do go to heaven. This was one of the greatest gifts any dog could leave behind.

What Could Be Greater?

Living life was painful without Erikka by my side. But whenever I was feeling alone, or thinking about her passing, I found comfort and even hope remembering those words, spoken to me at her death bed: "SHE WILL BE REPLACED WITH SOMETHING MUCH GREATER." Now I knew that it was God or a messenger from God who had spoken. That meant I had a "knowing" that what I'd heard would come to pass. The questions now were, what could possibly be greater, and how long would I have to wait?

What could that something be? I knew it wasn't a material object that money could buy. Money can't buy a relationship like the one we had. Therefore, it meant an even greater relationship. I didn't see that happening in the form of a new significant other in my life because even the love for another person, a mate, is not necessarily greater than the love you have for a pet. The two are just different. I realize that may sound awful, but there is truth in the fact that the love we have for our pets can fill deep needs on a level that cannot be fulfilled by people. There is a very special union, a form of love that is only available to us through the love of a pet.

For years I looked for the right words to identify why the love we feel for our pets is so special. I finally arrived at an explanation .....

An Explanation

What is it about a pet's love
that makes it unique from all others?

Why do we trust their love
when we struggle to trust the love of others?

How are they so easy to love?
Why such a healing love?
Can you explain it to me?

Could it be ...

Since we were created as imperfect human beings,
it is difficult for us to love imperfections.
But animals ...
were created in simple perfection.

Could their perfection,
   be a reflection of God
      and that is
         the connection?

In God's family we are one.
We are taught that God loves us with all our imperfections.

Through God's creatures, we know this to be true.

So, what could be "GREATER?" I knew it couldn't be another German Shepherd. Though I loved the breed, Erikka was more like a daughter than a dog. Maybe it would be something altogether different—like a horse, or a monkey! In either case, I was in no position to buy a new pet, and besides, when the time was right it would present itself to me. Of course, there were those moments of doubting whether or not I had actually heard a voice. And yet, as crazy as it seemed, I knew I had.

In some ways, Erikka's death had come at an ideal time. She had lived with me in Phoenix for most of her life, and that was where she died. December 15, 1980. It marked the end of a chapter for me.

For some time, I had already been preparing to relocate and open a dog training business of my own. My employment contract contained a "covenant not to compete" clause for the entire Phoenix area. That left Tucson, where I didn't know anyone. I didn't know my way around town either—tough when your business involves going to people's homes. Then, too, my faithful co-navigator was no longer with me. I was lonely without her, and scared to be starting out on my own in business, but in January 1981, I loaded up everything I had and made the big move. In some ways, it turned out to be easier than I thought. I didn't have those painful memories of Erikka, triggered by everywhere we had been in Phoenix. But it was harder, too. Emotionally, I was able to move on, but practically speaking, I faced a new problem. On new appointments, whenever I got to the part where I had to explain what a client's dog would be learning, Erikka wasn't there to demonstrate. I'd feel lost without her for the first second, and then the tears would follow. I cried for quite a few new clients.

Life rolled on, and with it came new challenges. The dog training business is stressful financially, especially when you haven't become established and no one knows your name. But I hung in there and tried to make the best of things. I soon had a small staff of trainers working for me at Arizona Dog Training Academy, Inc., each one having come from a different background. I began holding trainers' meetings to get us all on the same page with the programs we offered.

One day, the topic was protection training. I had spent a full hour going over safety procedures and how to avoid getting hurt. At the end of the meeting, we all went over to the local guard dog service to work on protection exercises with some of our dogs. When we first arrived, being very safety conscious, I decided to go up and down the facility's runs to make sure all of the cages were securely latched. Dogs at a guard dog service always know when there is training happening in the yard. Once they hear the barking, they all want to come and join in.

I was walking along the cages, securing the latches from the outside, when suddenly I felt a horrible pain. A dog, having managed to get his teeth outside the cage, now had my finger in his mouth and wasn't about to give it back. When a dog latches on, and really means to do damage, it seldom reopens its mouth. He went into this sawing action with his teeth, and by the time I did get my finger back, there was only a bone sticking out at the end. He had bitten off the tip of my finger. After my one-hour lecture on safety, and in less than ten minutes at the kennel, I was missing the tip of my finger. I covered it up, not really wanting to look. By now, it didn't hurt anymore (also a good indication that I was better off not seeing). I only had to look at the faces of the people around me to know that it was bad.

That was tough to recover from. I still had business at the guard dog service. I was boarding some dogs there, and when I went to take care of them, my knees would start shaking. This was a new, deep-rooted fear I was going to have to conquer. It was the first time I began to ask myself if I was in the right business after all. There were days when I tried hard to imagine what other profession I might love. But the truth was, I knew then, as I know today, it's not just that I train dogs—I am a dog trainer. It's my gift.

Meanwhile, I continued to stay in contact with some of my dog training clients in Phoenix—in particular, Larry and his wife Jackie, whom I had met when they called about training their new puppy. Larry and I really hit it off and soon became dear friends. He even took a stab at being a dog trainer and came to work for the same company in Phoenix. It was Larry who introduced me to his dear friends in Tucson, who were also interested in training their own dog. They were happy to help me get my business going; in fact, I used one of their bedrooms for my first office location. So the business was launched and began to grow.

It was then that some of the personal trials and tribulations of my past seemed to be resurfacing to test me once again. The depression I felt as a teenager—the isolation, the disliking myself for being gay, the belief that no one would ever love me—was a place I never wanted to visit again. Also, since I was committed to making a difference in the world for others, one way of doing that had been to live my life as honestly and as responsibly as I could—to be a shining example of a good human being and to NEVER deny my gayness. I was out of the closet for good!

However, at the age of 28, I started once again questioning the appropriateness of my gayness— not questioning the fact that I was attracted to women but whether it was appropriate! One crisis followed another, and I was thrown back into doubting myself.

*The first crisis that sent me into a meltdown hap-
pened when I went to visit a well-known figure in the
dog world who was living in California at the time.
Her celebrity status was the result of a book she had
written. I had been in contact with her and struck up
a good relationship over the phone. She knew that I
was in the business of buying dogs, training them,
and then selling them as trained dogs. She told me
that she had some very nice German Shepherds I
might be interested in and welcomed me to drive
out to California to visit and purchase a few dogs.
She welcomed me to bring one of my trainers with
me since I really didn't want to make the trip alone.
We were also invited to stay at her house.*

*I had really been looking forward to the trip,
but once we arrived we discovered a picture very
different from what she had painted over the phone.
The dogs that she had talked about were all mixed
breeds, which was not what I was expecting. We were
also horrified over the condition of the kennels. It
was absolutely sickening. I don't remember all the
excuses she gave for the place being so disgusting,
but my trainer Judy and I handled it by rolling up
our sleeves and spending a full day or two trying
to get the place civil. We worked our butts off.*

*As we were getting ready to leave with the dogs
I had selected and paid for, our host announced*

that she appreciated the help, but please … "never contact her again." She said she realized that I was gay and felt it was an abomination against God. She further told me that with her celebrity status she just couldn't afford to be associated with a homosexual. I was humiliated. Judy was equally shocked but had been spared the scorn, as she was heterosexual. It hurt … that's all I can say. It really hurt.

Shortly after that, the woman I was in love with at the time started going to a church for Jehovah's Witnesses, whose religious doctrine taught her that homosexuality is a sin. Needless to say, she broke off our relationship. It was a "God-says-homosexuality-is-wrong" thing with her, too! There were a few more incidents of the same type that finally drove me to my knees, once again humbled, asking: "God, is it wrong? Is my love wrong? Should I try being with a man? Is that really what you want?"

Larry would sometimes come down from Phoenix on the weekends. He and Jackie were now divorced, largely because they couldn't have children. Larry didn't like being alone, and I would try to line up dates for him. One Saturday we were at a party where the usual fare of pot and booze was accompanied by the newest craze—quaaludes.

Being high on quaaludes is very similar to the feeling you have when you are intoxicated with alcohol ... magnified by ten. If you take quaaludes and drive, for example, you *will* crash your car; it's just a fact.

When the party was over, Larry ended up staying the night at my house. A girlfriend of mine named Yolanda, who was visiting that same weekend, was also staying at my house. I had known Yo Yo since we were kids living in Bombay, India. Her parents had been stationed there at the same time mine were. Despite my *best efforts*, I could not get Yo Yo (who is *very* heterosexual) to share the bed with Larry, so I had to. Well, you guessed it. All the components were in place, and Larry was in the mood. I decided to be "open minded" to a new experience—especially if what everyone was saying about God's approval was right!

Because I loved Larry as a dear friend, I was not grossed out. At the same time, it was wonderfully clear to me—in an instant—that this was not natural behavior for me. My quandary was resolved and I would never have to feel guilty or wrong again! Behaving as if I were heterosexual was unnatural—a lie.

Being with Larry gave me compassion and understanding for those heterosexuals who declare homosexuality bad because it's not natural. It makes total sense to me now that if you are heterosexual, the thought of being with someone of the same sex would seem unnatural. Of course it would. That's as it should be. This is Nature's way of letting you know your true sexuality. It is not, however, a license to believe that what's right for you must be right for everyone else. Each of us is born with the gift of knowing what is right for ourselves—through discovery. Living a life that honors God requires listening to our internal voice and following the unique calling we each receive. This inner voice is our guide to inner (and often outer) peace.

So I now had this newfound peace—which was good because I was about to embark on a trip to visit with my family. My parents, then stationed in Ghana, Africa, were planning a trip back stateside, to stay nearly a month. Whenever Dad accepted a job in another country, he would typically be stationed there for at least three years, so they would sell their house here and pack up all their belongings. On this home leave they decided to stay with my sister, Kathleen, who was living in Virginia Beach. I was flying out to see them. Kathleen called to discuss my trip and dropped the bombshell.

"Oh, by the way, I told Dad that you are gay!"

"You what?"

"Yeah, I told him. What's the problem?"

"After all of these years of your telling me not to tell him and then you went and told him!"

I wanted to choke her, but that was Kathleen. I knew I would have to bring up the subject in some diplomatic way and at least let Dad know that I knew Kathleen had told him. My chance came one evening when we were all out to dinner together. I started.

"So, Dad, Kathleen told me that she told you I am gay."

He said something like, "Yes."

I continued. "Well, there's something else I really want you to know."

"Yes …" he said again, in a "Go ahead" sort of way.

"When I was young and I always got into so much trouble, you would ask me why I was doing this to you and Mom. I hope you understand that I was never trying to hurt you. I was having a terrible time and I didn't care very much about myself."

He stopped drinking his soup and looked at me.

"That makes sense." Then there was a long pause. "So how do you feel about yourself now?"

"Great!" I flashed him a big smile.

And that was that. We went on to talk about something more comfortable for everyone else.

I stayed in Virginia Beach only a few days. On the flight back to Arizona, I was walking down the aisle to use the restroom when I felt something swoosh through my body. It was not exactly like the plane had turned or suddenly dropped in altitude; it was more subtle than that. I want to say it was ... like a spirit ... had passed right through me. That's when I heard a voice again—my second one, mind you! This one was childlike, female, and giggling.

"You're pregnant."

Right! We're 35,000 feet up, and suddenly we're replaying the Annunciation? I think not!

I sped back to my seat and tried to dismiss what I thought had just happened. I declared it impossible. Yet ... just like the time before, I knew better.

Back on the ground (but definitely not grounded!), I tried to go on as if everything was normal. A few weeks later I was getting a haircut, and all of a sudden I was sick—throwing-up sick. Naturally, the hairdresser and I thought I had the flu—in fact, she was actually a little put out with me for showing up sick, but I hadn't had any other warnings or any other symptoms. Then, a few days later, I realized that I had not had a period yet. Normally, I never even thought about stuff like that. Well, why would I? But subconsciously, I guess, there was a little voice inside telling me to notice that I hadn't had a period yet. Plus, there was that getting-sick-at-the-hairdresser's experience. Wait, this was stupid. After all, Larry had been tested by a doctor. He was sterile. Besides, I had just gotten over my period the day before he and I were together. No way could anything happen!

One morning Katherine, my office manager, came in and sat down at the kitchen table.

"Karyn, there's something I need to tell you."

She blurted out that she thought she might be pregnant. As soon as she said it, the words poured out of my mouth too.

"I'm afraid I might be pregnant too."

Was that really me telling her that?

She was going in for a pregnancy test that afternoon, so I gave her a sample of my urine and asked her to take it along. I wanted to get this silly notion of being pregnant out of my head and get on with my life. An hour later, she called me from the doctor's office.

"Well?" I said a little rudely.

"They won't tell me your results, so you talk to them," she shot back.

Silence. What was taking so long?

I heard someone grab the phone and start to ask, "Is this Karyn?"

"Yes, this is she."

"The test results are positive."

"Huh? I'm sorry?"

"The results are positive. You're pregnant!"

"Thank you," I said and hung up.

I had just sent my urine along with Katherine so that I could get the silly notion out of my head! I never dreamed I was actually pregnant. After all—that would be impossible, right?

It didn't take very long for the news to sink in. I was pregnant. It truly was an "ah ha" moment. At last, I knew this was it—"SOMETHING MUCH GREATER."

Chaos

It was like someone had come along and stuck me in a dress and said, "You're not only a girl, but you're a pregnant girl!" Talk about needing God in your life! Talk about a big "This Just Can't Be!"

My first vivid childhood memory goes back to one Sunday morning watching my mother as she held up what she thought was an adorable little dress on a hanger. I was sure that this dress was for my older sister ... until she started eyeballing me. I knew that this was a big mistake, but she seemed to be intent on making me wear it. I put up a good fight. Then she had my father join forces, and I remember my father trying to hold me in his lap and help my mother get that dress on me. I was traumatized by the ordeal and remember screaming, crying, and

trying to fight them off. I could not understand WHY my parents were trying to put a dress on me. I can still see my parents looking at each other in total dismay, not understanding at all why I was so upset, and I was way too young to try to explain it to them. I just <u>knew</u>, from deep down in the core of my being, that I did not belong in a dress!

Some people would have described me as a typical tomboy, playing with what was then labeled as "toys for boys." I loved guns, cars, boxing bags, pogo sticks, riding my bike and playing with boys in the neighborhood. If I did play with dolls I was always the husband. I just knew inside that I really was a boy.

Despite my belief that I was going to be a boy, my mother naturally kept treating me like a little girl. Each morning she would start out by combing and styling my hair in a cute little girlish pixie cut. She would take her time, combing my hair towards my face in what she saw as a flattering hairstyle for a little girl. I would wait patiently for her to finish, and as soon as she would leave the bathroom, I would grab that comb, hit it with water, and start slicking my hair back the way it should be. I still remember standing on the toilet, looking in the mirror as I was redoing my hair, when my mom walked by the bathroom. Once again catching me red-handed, she looked at me this time with dismay and said, "You really believe that if you keep combing your hair that way, you'll be a boy someday, don't you?" With that being said she just sighed and went on her way. But that was the day I got it! I was always going to be a girl.

I learned to accept the idea and decided I would just have to make the best of it. Each birthday brought with it that very important moment of making my birthday wish. I always had the same two wishes. Wish number one was that I would never have big breasts so that I would never have to wear a bra when I grew up. The tell-tale sign for my mother that I had been messing around in her bedroom was when she would open her underwear drawer to find all of her bras poked in. I can still hear her calling, "Karyn, were you in my drawer again?" Wish number two was that I would have two big front teeth like my cousins. Both of those wishes came true!

Being pregnant, I couldn't have felt more like a fish out of water. How was I ever going to get through this? I had messed around ONCE and now the whole world was going to know. Gay me "doing it" with a guy … at best, I had a lot of explaining to do! In those first weeks, getting an abortion did cross my mind, but the fact was that this baby had been announced, and I knew it would be *a very bad idea to tell God, "No."*

Every evening I would go outside and sit on the tailgate of my pickup and smoke. One night, I got the feeling that I wasn't alone out there. I could sense the presence of what seemed like three little entities ... spirits ... hovering nearby, watching and being with me, considering me, deciding amongst themselves which one would have me for a mother. This began happening daily, and as the weeks rolled on, I realized at some point that there were only two. How did I know? I just knew. And it seemed as if they were having a debate as to which one should be my child. And then there was only one—a single little spirit joining me in my tailgate meditations. Then the visitations stopped. I understood that the soul who had been visiting me outside had now moved inside ... and was living in me.

Telling everyone in my life that I was pregnant was a very humbling experience ... and just the first of many to follow. I had to call my mom, who was still in the States. Another bombshell delivered by the daughter who had already caused considerable grief. My poor parents! Soon enough, though, my mom might be able to get her former wish: "I hope one day you have a kid just like you." Maybe that possibility along with being a grandmother would make her happy.

"What am I going to tell your father? You finally had the big talk with him, telling him that you're gay, and now I have to go back to Africa and tell him that you're pregnant?" We both saw the humor in that one. I could tell, though, that she was almost as embarrassed as I was … at least in the beginning.

My sister, on the other hand, was 100 percent there. In fact she told me, in no uncertain terms, that if motherhood was beyond me, she would take the baby and raise it herself. Ironically, sadly, my very heterosexual sister wanted nothing more than to have a baby, but had been unable to. Although there was no way I was going to take her up on her offer, it was comforting to have her on my side.

I had not dated anyone since the last girlfriend left me and became a Jehovah's Witness. But now I was feeling very vulnerable because of my new condition and was open to being in a relationship once again. Breaking my own work ethics, I got involved with a woman who was working as one of my dog trainers. I had known she was interested in me for some time, but her being an employee and the fact that she had never been with a woman before had helped me keep my distance. Any relationship is challenging, but going into a gay relationship with someone who has never actually dealt with that possibility in herself adds to the complexity. Chris seemed like just the support I needed—very feminine and actually more excited about the pregnancy than I was. It would be an understatement to say she helped me through the entire process. To this day, I still thank God for her during that time.

My first visit to the obstetrician was a nightmare. Sitting in the waiting room with a bunch of pregnant women who looked like they could give birth at any moment was almost more than I could bear. Was I going to look like that? How could I stand it after a lifetime of "choosing" the slim, athletic, boyish figure I'd always had?

"When was your last period?" the doctor asked.

"I don't keep track," I replied. "Why do you want to know?"

How annoying, especially after that highly uncomfortable examination. Anyway, why did it matter? The doctor seemed equally frustrated with me as he explained that he was just trying to determine when the baby would be born.

"Well, why didn't you say so? No problem! The baby was conceived on January 9th around 2:00 a.m."

His mouth dropped open.

"You don't understand," I said. "I'm gay, and this was the last thing in the world I expected!"

I wanted him to know just how awkward this was for me. "How would you feel if, all of a sudden, someone told you that you were pregnant? Because that's how I feel right now!"

He stared at me like I was some sort of alien. Needless to say, we did not have instant rapport.

Chris had to shop for my maternity clothes, something I could not bring myself to do. I wore regular clothes until I was ready to burst, and when I finally had to put on my first maternity shirt, I cried. It was just like I was being stuck in a dress again, knowing everyone would laugh at me. I refused to step outside of the house. To tell the truth, my friends were in a bit of shock, especially my buddies living in Phoenix. I heard that the word went around: "Who's the last person on earth you can imagine being pregnant?" People would think for a moment and then answer, "Garvin?" Then they'd just go nuts.

Larry was also pretty embarrassed. Poor guy! He had been married twice, and his last wife had been consumed with wanting a baby. They'd been trying for some time, but the doctor told him his sperm count was too low. That was a big part of the reason she divorced him. Finding out that her husband's lesbian friend was pregnant by him must have been tough. And Larry was also dealing with the fact that after being with him I knew, and I let him know, that I would never need to be with another man again. Though he understood my elation, he had a difficult time not taking it personally. Still, he was as supportive as he could possibly be.

My folks were having plenty of problems of their own. The Ghanaians were not happy that Firestone owned the tire plant. They felt it should be totally owned and run by Ghanaians. There was so much upheaval there that it became unsafe for my parents to stay. Firestone decided to send all of the Americans back home to the States. With no positions open in Des Moines, my father was offered early retirement. He decided to accept their offer and to come to Tucson to help out with his first grandchild. I found an apartment for them, and by the time they arrived, I was in my eighth month.

Being pregnant for anyone has its "funny" parts, like waking up in the morning and realizing that you're sleeping next to your stomach. Or one day discovering that you can't see your feet when you're standing up. Or having to admit that at 28, your arches have fallen from all the extra weight! These were problems for people who were really old or fat and out of shape—they weren't supposed to happen to me. But for this oversized pregnant lesbian, "funny" was the order of the day.

Not being your average heterosexual, feminine kind of girl anyway, I had not one whit of sense about maternity—or how to deal with it. Even at eight months, I was still running around—or trying to—in a body that, in my mind, couldn't possibly be pregnant, doing everything—or trying to—that I had done before, like fixing the evaporative water cooler on the roof. I got up all right, and did the job just fine, but then I couldn't get down! Somebody had to come and help my giant stomach down the ladder!

Or the time I decided to ride the Ferris wheel at the carnival. Why not? I had always loved the sensation. So Chris and I got in this little cage, which was connected to a lot of other little cages, and the contraption started spinning up in the air while our personal cage was doing its own revolutions as well. Wouldn't you know, all of a sudden we stopped at the very top and were hanging upside down. The damn thing was stuck and we were up there for a long time—long enough for me to experience some real fear and some very real pain. What kind of a jerk would even let a pregnant woman get on in the first place? And what kind of a stupid pregnant woman would try? Well, I was that one in a million, and I certainly paid for it that day.

Some women handle pregnancy as a special state of being—they take good care of themselves, and they love being doted on and being given preferential treatment by others. Me? Not at all. I found the process of physical expansion uncomfortable and inconvenient. For example, I'd show up at a client's house to work with the dog. I was a trainer, so that's what I had to do. Now, my belly was really big—bigger than average, because I'm a small-framed person. I'd ring the doorbell, and they'd sort of stand there and stare. They were supposed to hand over their giant dog—an Akita, or Rottweiler, a dog big enough to jerk me around … literally. Sometimes they'd just keep standing there, and finally I'd have to say, "Hello! Could you let me have the dog, please?" I'll never forget that look.

Chris was my hero throughout the pregnancy. I never knew how to cook—still have no desire to learn, for that matter. One of my biggest fears about being a mother was how I was going to feed a child. Chris saw me through my cravings for steak and cream of wheat. I just couldn't get enough of either ... might explain some of my hugeness.

She went to the childbirth classes with me. I had decided on natural childbirth because it was all the rage at the time, and because it was cheaper. I certainly had no health or maternity insurance. I learned to regret my brilliant decision on THE morning, when I woke up at 5:00 a.m. with contractions. It was already two weeks past the due date the doctors were predicting, so even *I* could figure out that this was the day. I called the doctor's office only to find out that he was out of town, but there'd be another doctor at the hospital and I didn't have to worry. I worried anyway.

Since I knew I wasn't going to take any pain medication, I was prepared with my marijuana to get through it. Another very bad idea! It slowed everything down. I was in labor for at least eighteen hours! We finally drove to the hospital late that evening when the contractions were closer together. Silly me, I was trying to delay being in the hospital any longer than necessary to save money. Sure, there was a doctor on staff, but he was pretty useless. As is so often the case, the nurses and Chris actually delivered the baby.

At 10:54 p.m., it was finally over. I had a baby boy, with *red* hair, the newest heir to the family name … Robert Michael Garvin. They put him into my arms right away and I held him tightly to my chest. He stared directly into my face, as if he were telling me something. In that moment, I knew that he knew that I was the one he had been living inside. He recognized the voice he had heard talking to him for so many months. Imprinting at its finest was taking place.

Again, as if I had orchestrated this to be the best it could be, both my parents and my sister were present for the birth, and my mother and father were elated. Here was the boy they had always wanted. I wanted to leave the hospital that night, but they told me I had to stay. In the early morning hours I had my first experience with breast-feeding. How weird was that? You'll just have to imagine what it was like for this tomboy. Yet, it also seemed quite natural.

I really wasn't expecting to see Larry so soon, because he was living in Phoenix, but I was mistaken. Chris had called him, and when I arrived home from the hospital early the next morning, he was there, eager to hold his son. From that very first day, all of the people to whom that baby boy meant so much surrounded us.

Grace

Thus began a new phase of my life, learning to be a mother and a parent. Once again, every day felt like Christmas with each day bringing a new gift—first smile, first laugh. What amazed me the most was how incredibly beautiful he was.

Thank goodness for my parents. They went shopping and bought him all new clothes. They embraced him, helped with taking care of him and loved him as their own. This was their grandson. Chris was tremendous as well. Her motherly instincts were natural and I could not have asked for a better partner. If only I hadn't needed to get back to work right away—it would have been nice to just be with my new son for a few days. For that loss, I was a little resentful but overall I was very grateful.

Time went on, and Robert grew more handsome and more beautiful every day. I remember waking one morning and looking at him. I was in Phoenix, visiting, staying at a friend's house. She came in the room and said, "Karyn, your baby's awake." I had put him to bed in a playpen next to me, the night before. There he was, with the morning light shining all around him: his beautiful red hair, his face peaceful and glowing. He was no less than breathtakingly beautiful to me. I had only seen that kind of beauty, the kind that brought tears to my eyes, once before in my life. Of course that was another time—a moment when I was looking at Erikka.

It's amazing how fast a nearly immobile infant becomes a rapid crawler. They go through a stage where they touch everything, and everything they touch goes straight into their mouths. It's a marvelous growth period that can drive a parent nuts. Unless crawlers are "penned up" they take 100 percent of your time. When they are out of the playpen, their tiny hands are in constant motion, grabbing and stuffing. It requires a steady stream of prevention that is difficult to handle.

Any dog trainer knows you can't get mad at your child and continuously say, "No." It's not good for the psyche—of man or animal. One day the solution appeared. Robert and I were at my mother's apartment, and I took him down to the swimming pool. He was wearing those little blow-up "swimmies" or "water wings" that you put on babies' arms to keep them from sinking.

I had taken him out of the water and set him on a towel in the grass. I had not yet removed the swimmies, but he began to crawl off the towel and started grabbing the grass. When he went to put the grass in his mouth, he couldn't! The swimmies blocked his arm from being able to bend enough to get it there. Hallelujah! I watched with amazement and delight. He could pick up whatever he wanted, but he couldn't put it in his mouth. And it didn't seem to frustrate him. It was just, "Oh well, I'll pick up something else." He was completely happy going through all the motions and totally okay that nothing ever made it to his mouth. Now I could take him out in the yard with me when I picked up after dogs and didn't have to watch his hands every second. When I had to be on the phone, the safety net of swimmies were on his arms. What a relief! He wore swimmies a lot!

My dog training business was home-based at that time. Customers called in, and either I or one of my trainers would go to the client's home for a private lesson. A lot of my time was spent answering the phone and tending to the dogs that were living with me. As I mentioned earlier, I was also in the business of purchasing dogs and then training them in obedience and protection. The idea was to have them ready to be placed as fully trained protection dogs. I was also breeding German Shepherds. Needless to say, there was a lot involved with taking care of the dogs and it included a lot of cleaning. I had to figure out a better way to become a successful working mother. My parents were able to baby-sit quite often, but there were still those times that Robert had to go to work with me.

It wasn't long before I needed and acquired an office location. Things were getting better; business was growing. But I was still a pothead, plain and simple.

Some people say you can't be addicted to marijuana, but I was. Getting high was the first act of the morning, along with a cup of coffee. Then I would shower to wash off any odor. A little Visine in the eyes to "get the red out" and I was off to work. That was my routine. I had been smoking marijuana daily since the age of 17. Of course, I didn't think there was anything wrong with it; people who engage in this behavior generally surround themselves with others who do the same thing, so it appears to be normal.

Robert went quickly from crawler to toddler and said his first word: "Dog." No surprise there, huh? It was clearly a love affair between my baby and my four-legged friends. I wasn't at all worried that he was getting too much exposure to dogs until he started acting like one.

One morning, I stood watching out the window as Robert and the dogs played. There were probably five or six dogs trailing one another, and Robert was running at the back of the line. The lead dog stopped and urinated, the next dog came up and stopped where the first dog had, took a long hard sniff, then marked over the first dog's spot. Along came the next dog, and then the next, all doing the same thing. The whole time Robert was waiting patiently at the back of the line. After the last dog, here came Robert. My heart lurched. He leaned over, put his head down, and sniffed just like all of the other dogs had. Oh God, what next? Without squatting or even lifting his tiny leg, he just hesitated for a moment and ran off behind them. Perhaps the critical threshold in the difference between dogs and people?

He did go through a period when he always wanted a leash attached to the back of his pants; it was his tail. And he was mighty determined to eat dog food. One day I decided to quit fighting it, and I just served him a bowl of kibble. He ate the whole thing. Fortunately, it cured him. He didn't get sick or anything, he just never asked for it again.

When the time came when people would ask: "Little boy, what do you want to be when you grow up?" Robert's answer was: "I want to be a Rottweiler." Then too, one of his favorite games was, "Train me. Train me." I would give him all of the dog-training signals: "Sit! Down! Come!" He loved going through the commands. Generally, that was fine with me, even cute, but sometimes I was a little embarrassed by his doglike behavior—perhaps more so because of my role in his deep immersion in that environment. But I also had to accept things as they were. This child had been "announced" to me, so I knew God would get us through.

It became pretty routine to take Robert to work with me. We had dog beds that were a perfect size for crib sheets. So when it was time for his nap, I just moved the dog out of the bed, slapped a sheet on it, and voilà, instant nursery! One day I was teaching a class when Robert woke up and toddled into the doorway. My back was to him, but I flashed him a hand sign and he knew exactly what it meant. He froze. I signaled him to stay, and he did just that. He sat by the edge of the room and never moved for the whole class. I never even turned around to check. The class continued without interruption, but I did notice the others in the room staring at him. They couldn't believe that this baby responded to hand signals and was as obedient as any well-trained dog could be.

Another Robert story. Actually, it's more of a confession. I was boarding dogs in our home, and Robert caught on pretty early that the dogs would come and stay for awhile and then disappear. Well, one day, he was wondering about this particular dog he liked—we'll call her Sally—and he asked me where the dog was. "Well," I told him, "here's how it works. The dogs come here; we do all the training. Sally's all potty trained, she knows how to go outside, she's obedience trained, and now she gets to go to a new home!"

Then I don't know what came over me.

"Speaking of which," I ventured, "you're potty trained …"

He looked at me in horror. "No!" he shrieked. I shouldn't have, really, but it was such a moment, and I couldn't resist.

Robert's first full sentences at about age two were questions—important ones like: "Is the hot wire on?" He was referring to the electric fence around the yard. I told him that if he touched it, it would hurt, and like all healthy, curious kids, he had to find out for himself. So I'd hear him yell from time to time when he played out in the back. But I left him pretty much alone about it—it couldn't really harm him, just smarted. Then there was Chris's little Lhasa Apso, who snarled and showed her teeth to the baby. I warned him, "Robert, she's going to bite you!" But he wouldn't leave her alone, so he felt those teeth more than once. The dog was not inappropriate; in fact, she was a perfect teacher. Soon enough, my son began to believe me when I warned him that something would hurt.

As much as I loved my baby boy, as beautiful as he was, and even with all of the joy he brought, something inside me knew it still wasn't greater than the love I felt for my first dog, Erikka. It felt like trying to compare apples to oranges. I would think about those words I'd heard the day she died: "SHE WILL BE REPLACED WITH SOMETHING MUCH GREATER." I loved my son. I adored my son, but I sorely missed Erikka. As much as I wanted my feelings for Robert to be as deep and rewarding as my relationship was with her, it just wasn't the same. I had loved that dog as much as a person could love anyone or anything. And I would ask myself: "How is this GREATER?" Then I would tell myself to just be patient.

I was a happy person. I loved my relationship with Chris. My parents liked her and welcomed her as one of the family. She continued to work with me as a dog trainer, and she did an excellent job with that, too. I couldn't have planned it any better myself. Coming from a homosexual perspective, this was as close to the way it should be as I could ever have imagined.

Except for the challenges in motherhood, things were pretty good. In fact, the people working for me were great. I had the ideal support system all around. My sister decided to move to Arizona to be closer. The whole family came together as a result of my baby boy. I was building my business and loving my work. I had big dreams for the future and I was on my way.

And then, one night, I had this dream. In it, I was sitting on a concrete floor in a stone-walled room in front of a giant fireplace. The room was cold and empty, with not even one piece of furniture. I was feeling lost and sad because I had been stripped of all my worldly possessions. Everything had been taken away. I had nothing left. Then, there was a loud, thundering knock at the door. Three pounding knocks to be exact. They echoed through the

*empty room. I got up and went to the huge wooden door; it swung open slowly to reveal a brilliant, blinding light. Even though I was blinded, I knew someone was there. And this someone was male. I was overwhelmed with the feeling of love radiating through me along with a new knowing that **everything**, would always, be okay.*

Impossible to describe or explain any further, but I got the message that a man would be coming into my life and that everything would always be okay. I woke up in a state of unquestioning peace—except that I was a little mystified. This was no ordinary dream. The powerful feeling of overwhelming love stayed with me for days.

Of course I had to tell people about the dream because I couldn't shake the feeling I was left with. No one offered me any interpretations. So I waited in a state of expectancy—for what, I didn't know. And then, my life came crashing down around me. It all happened over the next thirty days.

It started when Paul, who was one of my best trainers, suffered a terrible car accident, receiving a severe blow to the head. Paul had been with me from the start when I first moved to Tucson. His father was a veterinarian and Paul knew he wanted a career with animals as well. Since he was not interested in following in his father's footsteps, he rode with me on numerous appointments to explore the possibility of becoming a dog trainer. I was a mentor for him as a dog trainer and we became dear friends as well. In fact, I loved him like a brother.

He appeared to recover from the car accident, and the doctors couldn't find any brain damage to speak of. But, overnight, literally, he turned into a different person. He suddenly hated my guts and couldn't tell me why. We hadn't even had a fight. He just felt totally different towards me—that I was his enemy. This was my first encounter with someone who had a personality change as the result of a head trauma. We had to end our working relationship, and for me, it was a heartbreaking loss.

Then Chris became distant. I could tell something was going on, so I confronted her. She had fallen in love with one of her customers—a man. She had always dated men prior to meeting me. Now she needed to be back in a heterosexual relationship. While she had seemed fully present in our partnership, I still should have seen it coming because she'd never told her parents the truth about us. I had respected her decision to remain in the closet to her family. She was sure that they wouldn't understand.

Now I realized she was never truly comfortable with her gay side and she needed to move on. And boy did she ever! Within two weeks, she had rented another house and taken all of her belongings, leaving me absolutely nothing. When Chris and I had first combined households, I got rid of all of my furniture because hers was much nicer.

Now that mysterious dream was becoming a frightening reality. The house was empty, loneliness echoed on the bare concrete floor, and I had nowhere to sleep except on the carpeted floor in Robert's bedroom.

My heart was also broken for baby Robert, who was two-and-a-half years old at that point. He kept asking, "Where's Chris?" Whenever he saw a car that looked like hers, he would point to it and say, "Chris's car?" Then, as if it weren't bad enough, Chris never mentioned a word about me or our relationship to her new love, so we had no more contact. She disappeared, in total denial about the years we had been together. Ashamed of the past, she went on as if it had never existed. And she left Robert as though the love between them had never existed either.

To make things even worse, I had another traumatic situation going on at work. My trainers had always been on an Independent Contractor status. My company had been modeled after the dog training company where I had been an Independent Contractor in Phoenix. All of my trainers had signed contracts with me, reported their incomes to the IRS, and paid their own taxes. I had been audited in previous years and had never had a problem. Now, another IRS inspector appeared, and this guy had already made up his mind before he got there. He declared that all of my trainers should have been employees and that we owed employee back-taxes of approximately $40,000. I was sure it was a mistake and that the guy was just wrong.

My accountant went down to the IRS office with me, but they wouldn't listen. It was either pay up, or go to court. I had a third alternative—close up my business.

So there I was. Chris, my partner and second mother to my son, gone. All of my furniture, gone. Paul, my best friend and trainer, gone. And now my business, too! All within a month.

I got desperate and I got high. I was trying to understand the denial and rejection by those who had once loved me. Except for Robert and my immediate family, I was alone. They felt really bad for me, tried to comfort me, but there was nothing they could do. Somehow, that comfort had to come from within. Reaching out, I called an old friend who had actually been a dog training customer of mine in Phoenix. I had always looked up to Joanne. We weren't great friends, but I respected her and she liked me as her dog trainer. She was single at that time. We really never discussed our personal lives very much. She was probably at least ten years older than I was and just seemed to have her act together. She was into metaphysics and well-being, and she was also very spiritual in her own way. My little voice just nagged at me and told me I ought to call her. I was looking for some answers and hoping she might be able to give me the direction I needed.

We talked on the phone, and she was sorry to hear about my tough times. I also told her about my dream. She said she really didn't feel like she could give me advice, but she did have some books that she could send me that I might find helpful.

Within the week, I received a package from her containing three books. I don't remember the title of two of the books, but there was one in the package that I will never forget. The title was *Mary Magdalene*. I didn't know anything about Mary Magdalene then. The book described her life as a child, and how she ultimately became a prostitute. Then she meets Jesus, and there is a deep sense of how dear their relationship was. The story ends with Jesus being crucified on the cross. I was so naive; I didn't even see it coming. I wept and wept, and it was in that moment, reading that book, that I felt total loss—as if I had died on the cross with Him. Then I knew. The man who had come into my life and was capable of that kind of love, comforting me with the knowledge that everything would always be okay, was Jesus. All I had to do was open the door.

The Voice Said "GREATER"

Besides the IRS problem, business itself went from bad to worse. By this time, I had taken a leap of faith and moved the business into a larger building where we could offer indoor dog training. The building was also on a popular, high-traffic road, which I thought would help. When I made the move, I also believed that I had the financial support of a customer who had committed herself verbally. But she did not keep her commitment, and though I hung on to the bitter end, the day finally came when I knew I had to throw in the towel and close the doors.

Financially, I could not make ends meet. My house was going on the auction block. My truck, too, had been repossessed and, as fate would have it, was going up for auction the same day as the house. A benefit of closing the business at this point was that it also got rid of the dispute with the IRS.

My father stepped in and made a deal. If I could come up with the money for the truck, he would help bail me out with the house. Thank you, Dad! The money my parents lent me was to be paid back at a later date, and I certainly appreciated the help. I also knew that their financial support was fueled mostly by their concern for their grandson. If not for Robert, they wouldn't have even been in Arizona.

It was crushing to let go of a business that for more than eight years I had worked so hard to build. I had really hit rock bottom. And the problem wasn't my business, it was me. I had a little boy to raise and provide for, and I was not the role model he deserved. I had to clean myself up and start over. It was then and there that I started going to AA meetings and began to turn my life around.

So life went on. I cleaned myself up and started over. Raising Robert became more and more challenging as he grew older. I believe it was around the eighth grade when Robert really started getting difficult. It was as if, all of a sudden, he woke up one day caring about how he looked and how he dressed. Life with Robert changed for the worse that year. I went from being a parent to being a policeman. My mother's curse of, "I hope one day you have a kid just like you!" had come to fruition, and here he was.

He was constantly getting into trouble at school and putting me to the parental test on a daily basis. The school was calling too often, and he was messing with some of the same "stuff" I had used. Even AOL Inc. was calling because Robert had become a formidable hacker; he was in other people's websites, and generally being devilish. He was becoming a truly rebellious child—can't imagine the origins of that!—fighting the rules, making up his own.

One Monday, I was driving to Robert's school for the too-many-eth time, and I was furious—not afraid, mind you, but hopping mad. Again Robert's school had called, and again I had to go talk to the principal. I was really pissed; as I drove, I was hitting my steering wheel. This parenting stuff was not fun!

I was talking to God, as I often did, and I was dumbfounded.

"GREATER? Are you kidding? God, is *this* what you meant when you said Erikka would be replaced with something much GREATER?" That was when I got it! I heard it loud and clear. A voice in my head shouted back, **"The Voice Never Said 'BETTER' ... The Voice said 'GREATER.'"** What a difference! A difference that only someone who has loved a pet as dearly and deeply as I had loved Erikka would understand.

The way we love our pets is just different from the way we love people.

Robert has been a blessing from the beginning. I have no doubt that I love him as much as any mother can love her son. It's true that he brought our entire family together like nothing else would have. It's true that he is and will always be my most precious human relationship in this lifetime.

Today as I write, he is 27 years old. He works with me and manages our Invisible Fence® Brand[1] dealership for Southern Arizona. He's also my computer wizard, my web host provider, my graphic designer, my doggy day care web cam guy, and let's see … whatever else. He's my guy. We get to see each other almost daily.

Robert came into my life at just the right time; raising him required me to be a better person, and it seems like that never ends. The relationships we have with other people do help us strive to be greater. They make us greater when we make the right choices and learn to do the right thing.

There has still never been a dog that has touched me so or was better than Erikka, but I am happy to report that now, nearly 30 years later, I do have a close runner-up. His name is Luke and he is a two-year-old male yellow lab. He's fabulous … he's not Erikka yet, but he's fabulous. He goes to work and works with me every day. He's lying next to me now as I write. I believe he's heaven-sent too!

---

[1] Invisible Fence® Brand is a registered trademark of Invisible Fence, Inc.

Their Too-Short Lives

I couldn't count the times over the years that I've heard someone say, "No more dogs! It hurts too much when they die. That's it—no more!" I understand. I understand how hard it is, but I've also been around long enough and seen enough to know that the people who do start over are much happier. If you believe, like I do, that EVERYTHING happens for a good reason, then the same must be true of their too-short lives.

Luke

A letter I wrote to Luke

Oh Luke,

You're just a little over a year of age and I know you're a keeper. Lots of dogs pass by my way . . . rather, I couldn't even count the number of dogs that have passed through my arms, my training, and my caring, but none of them have been like you.

I love you, Luke, and it hurts already. I love looking at you, I love hugging you. I love your licks and being with you. You are a dog . . . you are a beautiful dog.

First I was looking for a working buddy and you passed. Not every dog will lie on their spot for endless hours watching other dogs get trained. But you, Luke, you lie there and watch, and I can actually see the wheels turning as you wonder what I'm going to teach today.

*Oh, the lucky person who falls in love with a dog for the first time! The **first** time we give our hearts away and love every minute of every day. This time around, I already know. I know from the beginning that you will be irreplaceable. I know from the beginning that you will be one of my greatest joys as well as one of my greatest losses. I know our time together will go all too fast. I know I will love you with all of my heart, and then I will have to say goodbye. I know when that day comes that God will be with us and that will bring comfort. I know that you will go to heaven, too. Knowing all of this in advance, I choose to love you, to let go and start all over again, as **this** is one of the greatest lessons in a human's lifetime. You, my dog, bring with you this gift. There's no love better than unconditional love.*   *Love, Karyn*

Acknowledgments

I feel so blessed knowing the people I am about to mention here. I am equally grateful for their wonderful dogs, which in most cases are what brought us together in the first place. I love doing the work I do, teaching people how to teach their dogs—helping them find harmony. It is my greatest joy, my abundance.

I do not consider myself an author, but rather a person with a burning desire to share a story. To begin, I would like to thank those who took the time to read my rough drafts and then gave me valuable direction with their comments. They helped me find my way: Barbara Brown, Alan Hamilton, Marla Motave, Moria Aicher, Cathy Rosenberg, Christina Garvin, Maureen Odenwald, Vicky Gutierrez, Kate Titus, Julie Darling, Elaine Provancha, Barbara Green and Kate Demeester.

Next, I would like to thank those with the gifts of writing and editing. Because of them, this story has found its way to you. Gail Martin, you, in particular, have helped me become a better writer, and I thank you! My special thanks also goes out to Rebecca Salome, Kathy Simko, Carol Calkins and Brookes Nohlgren.

How do I begin to thank my lifelong friend and well-known artist Diane Rath? Both my life, and now this book, have been blessed because of you. Diane created the painting for the cover of this book. Visit her website www.DianeRath.com to see more of her beautiful work.

My parents, I thank you for the opportunities you gave me as a child growing up. You provided me with amazing experiences that gave me much of the strength I have today. Mother, you were my first role model, teaching me how to love and care for animals. Dad, you were my greatest mentor, demonstrating to me what it means to have a strong work ethic. My sister, I thank you for being there and for all the support you have shown in my lifetime. You helped teach me how to be a girl!

To my son, words just cannot express my gratitude for you. This story is also in your honor.

To Erin, my significant other, thank you for standing by me and supporting me during this process. Life with you continues to make me a better person.

Most of all and every day I thank our one creator, our one God, for helping us to know His love thru each other and thru our divine canines.

I love you all and thank you,

Karyn

About the Author

Karyn Garvin refers to herself as a professional dog trainer and animal behavior specialist. There are only a handful of people in this country today who have been training dogs professionally for as long as Karyn has. "Professionally" being the key word here. This has been her livelihood, working at it six days per week for over 33 years. She was a professional dog trainer before it was really even known as, or considered, a profession.

As a young child, she moved with her family from Iowa to India, where she was deeply affected as she experienced the harsh realities and living conditions of that country.

She was left with a burning desire to help others, and to make a difference in the world. That experience, along with her college studies in behavior modification, contribute to making Karyn the trainer she is today.

Much of what drives Karyn is her commitment to saving pets' lives. Too many dogs and cats are relinquished by their owners because of behavioral issues that were not dealt with effectively. Karyn has discovered numerous opportunities to be instrumental in the field of pet training through her own inventive solutions. A key way in which Karyn measures her own success is by finding needs and filling them.

She found just such an opportunity on September 4, 1993. She was called to a customer's home to help them with a 13-year-old male poodle that had been marking in the house his entire life. What Karyn discovered was that all of the traditional methods of managing a male dog that marks would not work here. This dog had containment phobia, which meant that restricting his area had even more grave consequences for the owner. The wife had given up on trying years ago, but it was her new husband who came up with the idea of calling a dog trainer.

Karyn still remembers the very moment that the new solution came to her. She was sitting at the customer's kitchen table and asking the universe ... "God, what am I supposed to tell these people?" ... It was then that the idea flashed into her mind. In order to continue giving this dog its freedom, he would need to be diapered. Even this 13-year-old poodle was managed quickly after peeing on himself only three times!

Karyn then went on to create the first profession- ally retailed diaper for male dogs, the MarkOut® Wrap, and wrote the training manual *MarkOut® Marking*. She marketed this new product and method of training over the internet: www.MarkOut.com. Today, diapering a dog is a well-known method in the dog training world. The MarkOut® Wrap is still the male diaper of choice promoted by dog.com, the official pet partner for the American Kennel Club.

When pot-bellied pigs were all the rage in the 1990s, Karyn was inventive in running the world's first pot-bellied pig obedience class. She was there to help these pet owners learn how to live harmoniously with their new pets. You can still view the documentary video by going to her website: www.GarvinsPetPlaza.com.

In 1998, she expanded her dog training business to include the Invisible Fence® Brand solution, and became a dealer for Southern Arizona. As she grew familiar with the standard training procedure for Invisible Fence® Brand dealers, she found a need for a better way of training here, as well. Once she had developed, tried, and tested her new method of training dogs and cats, she shared her method of training through the Invisible Fence® Brand network. They adopted this new method of training, now known as the Perfect Start™ Method, and it is now used by Invisible Fence® Brand dealers across the United States. She was also fundamental in authoring the Perfect Start™ training manual. www.InvisibleFence.com

Soon after opening her Invisible Fence® Brand dealership, she discovered another need. As a dealer, she found her business servicing more "Houdini dogs" than she had ever encountered as a dog trainer. Owners, looking for solutions to keep their escape artists contained, often contact the Invisible Fence® Brand dealer. While the Invisible Fence® Brand is part of the solution, dealers still needed to understand the condition thoroughly in order to service these clients correctly. It was only then that Karyn coined the term "containment phobia" and created the distinction between containment phobia and separation anxiety. Her article was first published in the Invisible Fence® Brand *Dog's Life* newsletter in 2003. It was later published in the International Association for Canine Professionals *Safe Hands Journal*. This was an important advancement in the treatment for containment-phobic dogs. Prior to this, behaviorists were identifying the problem as separation anxiety, and the techniques for treatment would not work. A comprehensive source regarding containment phobia is available at: www.GarvinsPetTraining.com.

Her business today, Garvin's Pet Plaza, represents an integrated group of businesses, each one offering unique solutions to create harmony between people and their pets:

Garvin's Pet Training

Dog Day C.A.R.E.

Garvin's Pet Doors

Garvin's Online Store

See www.GarvinsPetPlaza.com for more information.

Dogs Do Go to Heaven!

Karyn prays that this book will fill a need in people's hearts for years to come. You can help her help others by sharing it with your friends.

Thank You!

Divine Dog Training: Taking the Integrated Approach

Divine Dog Training

Some people get inspiration from stories, some from nature.

Dogs find both inspiration and purpose in a job well done through training.

The dog's owner is inspired to be a great teacher and learns how to earn leadership.

The dog learns to love its owner even more.

—Karyn Garvin

Times have changed! It used to be that when people needed help with training their dogs it was a pretty straightforward process. There wasn't that much information out there, and people weren't as knowledgeable about training dogs as they are today. Thirty years ago people were actually surprised to learn that they shouldn't spank their dogs. Hardly anyone used crates, and dogs always got the family's leftovers after dinner. Restaurants weren't kidding when they handed out doggie bags for the leftovers. A person would actually be a little ashamed about taking food home from the restaurant for themselves rather than giving it to the dog.

Today I am more proud than ever to say that I am a dog trainer. It is a growing and noble profession. I am grateful for all of the celebrity dog trainers who have elevated our profession on TV. I am also grateful to all the brilliant trainers who have authored books, produced tapes and videos and marketed their creations to the public. Each one of them has made a contribution by motivating people to automatically assume that training their dog is a part of dog ownership. It wasn't always this way.

Now, new clients coming in for dog training are much more knowledgeable and have questions we need to sort through before we can even get started. There is so much information available, and much of the advice contradicts itself. One trainer professes one method and claims it's the best while another trainer says their way is the only humane way. For that matter, people are also being told that certain types of training equipment are cruel while other types are not. People are actually more confused than ever, not knowing what to believe.

For this very reason, I feel there is a need to consolidate the information into what I am calling the "Integrated Approach." The truth is, God created each person and each dog as an individual regardless of the person's race or the dog's breed. There are many roads that lead to a divine life with a dog. I am obliged to provide people with a number of solutions and then support them in choosing what is right for them. I'm looking forward to the day when I can say that I use the Integrated Approach, and people will know what I'm talking about.

One of my heroes is Richard Buckminster Fuller, who is best known for creating the Geodesic Dome. What I love about him was his inventiveness. Both he and I thrive on finding a need and then filling it. Here's what he said:

> "The Things to do are: the things that need doing, that *you* see need to be done, and that no one else seems to see need to be done."

Quite frankly, I worry about the number of trainers who are preaching that training methods should only include methods using positive reinforcement. I worry for all the dogs and pet owners for whom this won't work. I worry for their very lives. If someone told me years ago that I would need to take a platform for the positive nature of consequences, I would never have believed them. But such is the state of the dog training world today.

Richard Buckminster Fuller is also well known for making "synergy" a common term. Simply defined, it means that the whole is greater than the sum of the individual parts. Taking the Integrated Approach to dog training has the same synergistic effect by offering more solutions to more people. The definition of the word "integrated" is "having all its parts combined into a harmonious whole; coordinating diverse elements." Trainers who use integrated training techniques will have more tools in their toolbox.

The Integrated Approach

We believe that with the . . .

Right Equipment
+ Right Application
+ Right Technique
_____

Total: Success in Training™

Training equipment is an important part of a dog trainer's tools. All of the equipment that has been invented to date has a unique purpose in mind. I like to compare selecting the right equipment to:

The Fork The Knife The Spoon

Different Tools, Serving a Common Purpose

Yet each utensil will outperform the others
when it is selected for the task it was designed for.

One of the most legitimate complaints of dog trainers today is that people will buy a piece of training equipment and not know how to use it. This, more than anything else, has led to giving certain training tools a bad name. *Divine Dog Training: Taking the Integrated Approach* goes into great detail on this subject.

A master trainer using the Integrated Approach is experienced with a broader scope of training skills, all of which translates into saving lives. It is still true today that a large number of dogs are relinquished to shelters and killed because of behaviors that *the owner did not know how to manage.*

In Divine Dog Training, we learn not only how to manage our dog's behavior, but more importantly, *we accept responsibility for it.* The distinction between Divine Dog Training and other ways of teaching is in the very foundation of how we view the dog. Divine Dog Training offers the belief that the dog may just be God's finest example of unconditional love. Just as a human being is also a spiritual being, so is your canine also a spiritual being. The dog has a spirit and listens to its internal voice just as we do. Many of our value systems are different, yet we learn to coexist.

Another one of my favorite mentors is Dr. Wayne Dyer. He is well known for the saying, "When you change the way you look at things, the things you look at change." The dog was created perfectly with all of its abilities to bark, chew, mouth, hump, dig, lick and any other innate behavior you can think of. There is nothing wrong with jumping for joy! God did not make any mistakes when he created the dog. Divine Dog Training does not make the dog "wrong" for these behaviors. Instead, it places the responsibility on you, the dog owner, to show good leadership and manage situations accordingly.

All behavior is either innate or learned. Innate behaviors are never going away for good, but they can be managed. Only learned behaviors can be extinguished. Trying to teach a dog never to jump is about as ridiculous to me as a person who thinks their dog should never bark. When we argue with Mother Nature, we will lose!

Live your life accordingly ... according to what is appropriate at the time. If Bobby, your 12-year-old next-door neighbor, is coming to visit and he loves it and laughs and giggles when your dog greets him jumping and licking, just let it be. It's not as if killing their fun would erase your dog's desire or natural tendency to be a dog.

On the other hand, if it's Aunt Louise coming to visit, and she's 95 years old, and just your dog bumping into her could knock her down and possibly break a hip, then **you** need to show good leadership and manage your dog. There are numerous ways to do this, which are detailed in the book, but you don't get to holler, "*Sorry, Aunt Louise, that* *damn dog knows better!"* He doesn't know better, he is a dog. For those of you who actually believe he knows better, you have lost sight of the fact that he is a dog. Believing he knows better places the responsibility on the dog and sets you up for disappointment. Assuming you need to manage your dog's behavior will empower you. Once again, "When you change the way you look at things, the things you look at change!"

It should be liberating to be told you have the freedom of choice, and that consistency lies in whatever you say goes. When you say it's okay to be a dog, it's okay. When you know it would be inappropriate for your dog to jump on someone, you assume leadership by managing the situation and redirecting him. There can be freedom in the framework. Life will certainly be a lot more enjoyable for both of you.

Divine Dog Training is a new approach. The words we use create thoughts. Our thoughts about things are reflected in our behavior. Much of dog training at the present uses words such as "behavior problems in dogs" or "how to stop jumping up." Once again, this kind of language suggests there is a problem within the dog. It is an illusion and bad instruction to insinuate that anyone can *stop all jumping*. This just leads dog owners to believe that either they are failures or there's something wrong with their dog. (*"That dog should know better by now!"*) Remember, God created the dog perfectly.

Our ability to manage the dog's behavior is the solution. That is the goal of obedience training. Obedience training is a big part of the solution and deserves a lot more focus than it's been given.

I look at dog training as teambuilding. I often describe obedience training as a dance. Like dancing, if you dance with someone who's awkward, it's awkward. But when you dance with a great dancer, you feel like a great dancer. It's because they lead the dance so well. A dog trainer's goal in obedience training is to teach you, the owner, how to lead the dance gracefully with your dog; how to be a team. This includes teaching your dog commands that will be vital to you in moments of needing to redirect his natural tendencies.

We love our partners, our dogs. It's just the behavior that sometimes needs to change. When we redirect a dog's behavior, it can be about correcting the old behavior, replacing it, and then rewarding the new. The empowering attitude for teachers is that they are correcting behaviors. We can't become afraid of correcting and redirecting. Of course, positive reinforcement is our primary way of teaching. It's more rewarding for both of us. This entire dance of obedience training is to be led with love. That is Divine Dog Training.

I realize in advance that no book can ever take the place of working with a behavior specialist and master trainer. No book can ever coach you in the fine motor skills and techniques needed to lead the dance of obedience training. This book will, however, balance out what the world is telling you. It will take the Integrated Approach and coordinate the diverse elements into a harmonious whole.

I have a dream of dogs being seen as an asset in the world, becoming more welcome everywhere. I would like to see them be better trained, better able to go with us into stores and restaurants, and basically with us wherever we may go. Our time together is short and precious. I believe that transforming how we look at dogs will also make them more welcome. We could use more love everywhere.

I hope that what you have read feels right for you. If it feels right, then it is right! The root of the word "obedience" means "to listen." I often tell my clients that to be obedient to God means to listen to your heart ... that is, after all, how the universe speaks to us. I listen to my heart every step of the way. I'm looking forward to sharing what life, people and their dogs have taught me.

www.integratedapproach.com